FEED THE RIGHT PIGGY BANK

*A Mini Wisdom Guide for Aligning
With Right Opportunities That Honor Your Worth*

Alicia "WATERS"

Feed The Right Piggy Bank

Copyright © 2014 Alicia "WATERS"

All rights reserved. Except for use in the case of brief quotations embodied in critical articles and reviews, the reproduction or utilization of this work in whole or part in any form by any electronic, digital, mechanical or other means, now known or hereafter invented, including xerography, photocopying, scanning, recording, or any information storage or retrieval system, is forbidden without prior written permission of the author and publisher.

The scanning, uploading, and distribution of this book via the Internet or via any other means without permission of the publisher and author is illegal and punishable by law. Purchase only authorized versions of this book and do not participate in or encourage electronic piracy of copyrighted materials. Your support of the author's rights is appreciated.

Names, characters, places, and incidents are based on the author's own personal experience therefore names of persons and entities remain unnamed to protect the integrity of the story and the privacy of those involved. Any group or organization listed is for informational purposes only and does not imply endorsement or support of their activities or organization.

For ordering, booking, permission, or questions, contact the author. www.anwempires@gmail.com

ISBN-13:978-1494974084

ISBN-10:1494974088

Printed in the United States of America by Create Space

Feed The Right Piggy Bank

Dedication & Acknowledgment

This book is a general dedication to all who are on the journey of achieving their highest level of truth and worthiness for wealth creation.

I give thanks and acknowledgments to God and all who have made my evolutionary journey wealthy.

Feed The Right Piggy Bank

Table of Contents

Introduction

Which Right Is Right at The Right Time?

Partnering with The Piggy Bank

Choose Only Worthwhile Collateral Opportunities

Does Your Piggy Bank Have Wings?

Calculate Before Conception: Is This Wealth Creation Endeavor Worth It?

Which Piggy Bank Opportunity Is Top Priority? Go for The Golden One

Having A Now & Later Plan Goes a Long Way

Listen to Your Inner Money Wisdom

Being Rightly Seen

Conclusion

Feed The Right Piggy Bank

Introduction

There are three key areas where individuals often sell themselves short. The areas of time, value, and money. Often, this primarily occurs in the areas of relationships, professions, and recreation.

Those three significant areas are often abused, neglected or mismanaged. Mainly in the world of business, especially in solo-entrepreneurship, coaches, consultants or practitioners often trade dollars for hours. In turn, this results in a lack of effectiveness for leveraging time, value and money.

Time, value and money are areas that truly deserve to be respected and honored especially if we desire to see more abundance flow into our lives. Often, when any of these areas are abused as it relates to the work that we do, the question of worthiness needs to be addressed.

Examining your worth concerning every area of life is critical. Doing an honest inventory to assess how we are respecting time, value and money will provide us with a measurable tracking system of our worthiness.

If we desire to see greater manifestations flow into our lives, then we must begin to honor and value ourselves with time and money. It's time to stop selling ourselves short so that we can attract that which we desire.

Feed The Right Piggy Bank

Feed the Right Piggy Bank

Making daily decisions about best wisdom practices can be challenging at times, especially if we have already spent so much of our internal and external resources trying to accomplish our goals. *Feed the Right Piggy Bank,* is a mini handbook guide with concepts that aid and assist with aligning our efforts to divine right opportunities for making wise investments of our time and money that honors our worth.

Which Right Is Right at The Right Time?

I came across a question once on the facebook fan page of million dollar marketing coach, Kendall Summerhawk,where she asked the question; Are you more worried about doing things right, or doing the right things?

This is a question I ask myself often, in fact almost every other day when it comes to my personal affairs and especially as it relates to making business decisions. Trying to figure out which right is right can be a bit challenging at times.

I believe that there is a divine balance in having the ability to operate from both ends of the coin when necessary. The catch is trying to figure out which right is right at the right time. In the children's show Barney, there was a character named Baby Bop who sang a song once called, what should I do? When I don't know what, I should do?

So, what should you do? Which right is right? I've chosen to adopt a no "Wrong Way" approach by choosing what I believe that love would do in my current situations. This invites me to move out of stagnation, make my decisions right for me. There is no wrong way because love always chooses right.

Partnering with The Piggy Bank

Every day is a perfect day to partner with your piggy bank. This begins with making a new vow to yourself about honoring your worth by choosing to only engage in divine right inspired actions. Choose endeavors that are going to allow you to make the most of your time, earn what you deserve and invest wisely.

Partner with your piggy bank in the present by making a commitment that you will fill your bank account with worthwhile collateral. No more trading dollars for hours or giving away too much for too little. Your piggy bank is your intuitive partner who is ready to co-create the financial status that you desire.

Choose Only Worthwhile Collateral Opportunities

I'm sure most have seen the Klondike Bar commercial where they ask the question; What would you do for a Klondike Bar? Sometimes we have to ask ourselves what would we do to truly be financially successful.

This challenge is a true test of character and strengthens our resolve to see if we will sell our souls through blood sweat and tears to make a dollar or will we find ways to create income by not settling for less.

I have a concept that I call, worthwhile

Feed The Right Piggy Bank

collateral. This is where I challenge myself to only do work that is going to be worthwhile and lucrative. I've made a vow to myself to commit to truly honoring my worth on all levels. Therefore, I carefully examine how I'm going to spend my time as it relates to making money.

If it's not worthwhile, I won't even entertain it. By getting clear, the universe can help to do the research and orchestrate opportunities for you to embark upon.

Only choosing worthwhile collateral is not just about choosing great money making opportunities, it's about engaging in a holistic total well-being framework that will yield prosperous short and long-term success.

Does Your Piggy Bank Have Wings?

Are your financial desires or goals bringing you wings yet? Lamarck and his "wishing" theory stills hold true. He claimed that birds do not fly because they have wings, but they have wings because they wanted to fly. We need to ask ourselves regularly; Does my piggy bank have wings yet?

Every day we need to examine our activities to evaluate whether or not our efforts will help us to accomplish our short to long term goals. We should have quality goals that are soaring on opulent levels and bringing us the rewards of an abundant harvest.

It's time to take inventory of your piggy bank
Feed The Right Piggy Bank

profit strategies, along with mastering your inner game to see if you have truly partnered with your piggy bank in order for your efforts to deliver the results that you desire.

Calculate Before Conception: Is This Wealth Creation Endeavor Worth It?

Wise wealth building principles often consist of strategic intuitively aligned planning towards your financial goals. I've developed a concept called "Calculate Before Conception."

Before embarking on certain opportunities that could potentially increase my income, I ask myself, is this wealth opportunity worth it?

Several of us have had the experiences of jumping in to get rich quick scams or operations that desire for you to invest money up front in order to build a business under their umbrella only to find out that it wasn't what you thought.

Wise wealth building takes time, focus and goal setting to achieve the long-term results that are worth it. Calculate the opportunities that present themselves before beginning the co-creative efforts of engaging in something that is simply not worth it in the long run.

These are some of the thoughts that we should begin to entertain before quote on quote jumping into bed with a low-end opportunity.

Feed The Right Piggy Bank

Which Piggy Bank Opportunity Is Top Priority?

Go for The Golden One

There is an old saying that everything that glitters isn't gold. This implies that every shining golden opportunity that presents itself isn't always what it's cracked up to be. However, I believe that there are times when you have to have what I call the Olympic moment. Going for the gold is the only mentality that you can have on your way to achieving your highest levels of success in that arena.

The time is now for living our best life ever, a golden lifestyle. There are several opportunities that present themselves for us to act on, however, we must carefully evaluate those endeavors and make sure that we are feeding the right piggy bank.

Having A Now & Later Plan Goes A Long Way

I believe in having a now and later plan for almost everything. I know that you can't necessarily always plan one for everything, however, when it comes to leveraging time and creating lasting wealth, having a now and later plan goes a long way.

Having a now and later plan allows you to play on both sides of the track while continuing to move forward. Like the candy, Now & Later, you get to savor the moment while working in the present along with being at ease knowing that you have a follow-up system in place for advancement to support your efforts.

Feed The Right Piggy Bank

But you have to begin taking action in the "Now" on your goals and not choose to put things off until later. Having a "Now & Later," plan is like having insurance, if you should run into a situation that stalls you on your forward movement, then you might be able to bring forth some of your pre-planning insights from your later agenda to support you in the present.

Listen to Your Inner Money Wisdom

Decide to take some time out to listen to your inner money wisdom to gain clarity before moving forward with your wealth creation goals. In order to be in full alignment with your money path remember to always make sure that you're feeding the right piggy bank opportunities.

Like partnering with your piggy bank, connecting with your inner money wisdom intuitively allows you to hear what your piggy bank is speaking about on a higher level. This wisdom can help to launch you into the next realm of success that is more than you can imagine.

Slowing down, doing some deep breathing and tuning out all of the noise and information overload can assist you with opening up to a wealth creation idea that you would not have considered. Again, your inner money wisdom can reveal to you a higher perspective about a current idea that you're working on.

Being Rightly Seen

There was a time when I was very concerned about not being seen or having enough visibility on certain social media platforms as it related to being known as a brand in my business. At times, I felt like I was invisible and no matter how much talent I had, there just seem to be no real interest in who I was or what my services had to offer.

After doing several years of inner game work, I began to focus on seeing myself clearly first and not focusing so much on whether I was being seen or not. I learned to become visible to myself. I once heard a visionary and intuitive coach, Anya Sophia Mann say; "we do not need anyone to see us in order to be seen. We do not need anyone to hear us in order to be heard. We do not need anyone to feel us in order for us to feel ourselves."

I've come to realize that it's not about having so many people to see you that counts. It's about being rightly being seen by yourself and the right people who need to see you at the right time.

George Bernard Shaw, says; *"Better see rightly on a pound a week than squint on a million."*

Antoine de Saint-Exupery, says; *"It's is only with the heart that one can see rightly; what is essential is invisible to the eye."*

Feed The Right Piggy Bank

Both of those statements correctly express how wisdom combined with the passion that flows from your heart space is what aligns your inner sight to rightly see what your soul desires to express. This will eventually reflect in the outward manifestations towards your visibility.

Sometimes not being seen by others might be serving you. Again, you want to be seen by the right people at the right time. As mentioned earlier, the focus in the present should be kept on rightly seeing yourself the way that Source sees you.

Feed The Right Piggy Bank

Conclusion

Often, we question our true worth and what truly makes us valuable. Before we can truly come to understand the depths of that question, we need to understand what our true value is not.

Our true value is not in the amount of money that we have, the number of people who approve of us or in the illusion of being in a certain economic class. Nor is our value determined by our history or past failures or successes. Though we can learn from our history and our experiences from the past, we must understand that our value lies in the present moment of our "Now Potential."

We each have value to add and to gain in the "Now." There are unlimited possibilities that are waiting for us to explore. We will begin to experience new levels of our worth when we tap into our greater potential and share it with the world at large.

It's time to truly value ourselves, get out of the past or eliminate whatever is holding us back and realize that your value lies in our "Now Potential."

Feed The Right Piggy Bank

Reflections & Actions
(Record reflections from the reading to create a plan)

Feed The Right Piggy Bank

Reflections & Actions
(Record reflections from the reading to create a plan)

Feed The Right Piggy Bank

More Notes:

Feed The Right Piggy Bank

Reflections & Actions
(Record reflections from the reading to create a plan)

Feed The Right Piggy Bank

More Notes:

Feed The Right Piggy Bank

Reflections & Actions
(Record reflections from the reading to create a plan)

Feed The Right Piggy Bank

Reflections & Actions
(Record reflections from the reading to create a plan)

Feed The Right Piggy Bank

Reflections & Actions
(Record reflections from the reading to create a plan)

Feed The Right Piggy Bank

Next Steps for Continuation Resources:

Other Related Books on Amazon
Feed The "Write" Piggy Bank
This Little Piggy Went Marketing
I Like Frog Legs & Ham
Fattening Your Piggy Bank
Profitable Aha Moments

Creating Profitable Piggy Banks

Feed The Right Piggy Bank

For More Resources:

Visit:

www.profitablepiggybankspower.blogspot.com

www.amazon.com/author/alicianwaters

Or

To Book the Author

For Speaking Engagements

Email: www.anwempires@gmail.com

If you enjoyed this resource, please consider writing a review on Amazon.com.

Thanks & Blessings!

Feed The Right Piggy Bank

www.ingramcontent.com/pod-product-compliance
Lightning Source LLC
Chambersburg PA
CBHW070735180526
45167CB00004B/1768